History

History

Rodger Moody

sight | for | sight books
Boston   Eugene

History is published in a limited edition of 300 by
sight | for | sight books
2850 Baker Blvd.
Eugene, OR 97403

Library of Congress Control Number: 2014909131

First Edition

9 8 7 6 5 4 3 2 First Printing
Printed in the United States of America

Contents

PART II

for Dashiell and Julian

Part I

Lament

I've come back
to tell you about my life
along the river, about the rusty iron
bridge where my friends shot carp,
about how the cruelty of farmers
is the cruelty of fathers,
about how they lingered in hayfields
or drank beers on dark back roads,
or how they ached over small town girls
and summer shorts so tight each pair
shaped a butterfly between a girl's legs.

Memory Is the Rig

I can't erase Interstate 80 from memory. Or truckers. Truckers occupy my thoughts the way flowers and fresh air once did. Women. Women used to wake me in the morning, or the thought of women. The sweet curve of a woman's hips, surfaces of good use abundant on her back. In her eyes. The way to a woman's heart is on the back roads of her thighs; not the thighs really, but through the heart's ache to be thought of as more than just a road to pleasure. A man drives a rig across the body of the country and still he can't see his own nose. The soul's as wrinkled as my shirt and I've slept in what by all rights should be the last motel bed. And yet last night the light at dusk: unspeakable. it won't ever be like that again. If desire is asphalt then memory is the rig that carries me to my destination.

The Woods

for Dad

He could smell mushrooms
from the gravel road.

On the trail he'd use a crooked stick
to turn back the toadstools--

a boy I scurried up the hillside.
The steel mill almost forgotten,

we'd hike to a clearing
beyond the curving edge of a plowed field

to a fenced gully
where you had to step with care.

Our differences were more
than the rub between night and day.

We never saw the owner of the woods
or took anyone with us.

I remember the halved morels
soaked in saltwater

overnight in the refrigerator
then fried in butter on low heat

with eggs, black pepper.
I can hear the soft rain.

Small Town Lessons

When I was young
winter froze
into the biggest

icicle I'd ever seen,
the fang stood
seventy feet tall,

its tip biting
into a white ice field.
It was glimmering

ice piss, feces
and rubbers, a fetus
from a teenage

girl, tissue paper,
an inner map
of America, the last

beautiful thief.
I gazed over the edge,
my legs wrapped

around the short
steel pole stuck deep
in limestone. One day

a boy hung there
by just his two hands
until a man from

the waterworks
heard him pleading
with God.

Summer Winds

My father drives a Seville,
works in a steel mill,
plays golf at the local club.

He's nobody's boss but the man's
inside the blade of grass
on the fairway. Fields of straw

bend in my boyhood dream
of summer wind and working.
The bed on the carpet is mine,

not the hayloft. My father laughs
all round here, I often go mad
at night from the deep glare of wheat.

The Novice

I remember April rainstorms and winds so strong two tall spruce in
the front yard almost bent double. One afternoon the downpour was
so heavy I couldn't see the houses down the street. The gray couple's
house next to ours resembled a chicken coop and it held tight as
hard rain strummed the earth. The first time their grandson visited
he knocked early on our door. He stood in the yard and with two
fingers over one nostril he murmured something about *the farmer's
handkerchief* then blew a string of bright yellow snot that reached to
the uncut grass. He was thirteen, a novice teenager. That summer he
told me about a boy from his school's varsity basketball team who
had made him suck his cock until he exploded milky white semen
into his small, burning mouth. Indiana's seasons were always full
and fierce. My father's house was a perfect square with a large yard.
There was a woods across the street. One winter day I walked deep
into the woods. It had snowed six inches that afternoon. When I was
certain no one would find me I kneeled in the snow and tugged my
tight blue jeans to my knees. Nancy, or Nancy's apple cheeks, had
haunted me throughout the day's classes. I took off my wool gloves
and rubbed cold snow, handfuls of it, over my cock and thighs until I
was rock hard. Nancy felt close and distant at once. I held snow filled
hands around my cock and moved my hips in a slow motion reverie
as I jetted into the crisp February air of my remorse. Sixteen, and too
poor to ask Nancy out, this was as close as we would ever be.

A Matter of the Heart

I had a friend who forever rambled
about hay hooks and round bales
or how to build a grain bin
using jacks and ladders,
first the roof
then a ring at a time
or of the way dust settles
along the sides of gravel roads
and across the sun as it balances itself
on the horizon
or of the alien sense your bones get
at the sight of a cow
standing still on top of a hill,
only the endless blue sky
behind it,
about worn-out barns
and farmers who plow fields at midnight
their only company the moths
circling their tractor lights,
or of the landscape
and its importance to anyone alert,
I miss him
the way I miss hayfields
and flatbed trucks.

Grandma

had a faint mustache
and chain-smoked
                    like a man. I watched

    my mother's mother
eat a raw chicken gizzard
                    in her farm house
kitchen,

        we had just pulled the heads off

enough chickens to feed
everyone.
        After boiling them
we plucked the feathers as

easily as you might brush
rats
    from a young
girl's

                    tangled hair.

The New Kid

Elevated against flooding
the bridge stretches
over the muddy Wabash.
I'd park Dad's car close by
kiss girls beneath stars
dead now for centuries,
still I felt how light
can move sheer in space;
one night the new kid
after a basketball game
climbed to the top
of the iron supports,

it was winter and a chill
hung in the night air,
the girder another sixty feet
above the water he was yelping
about youth and the misery,
everyone was impressed
by his frank ways
and his sure grip on the cables
on his way back down.

Your Eyes Your Tongue Your Baptist Church

Deacon, you know
Jesus passed through these flatlands.
The Wabash River fills with top soil.
Chicken bones.
Sow jaws. Jesus
loves corn on the cob. Puts Bibles
in every farm house. Even in your wife's
new dress. Your eyes turn heavy
in dim light while Jesus sighs as he
rides your backbone to the spot where
ground opens its rock teeth to welcome you--your skull
the bell in the throat of a Bible.

The Experiment

The barn at my grandparent's farm
was old like they were, only
I had a younger aunt
and uncle. One sunny afternoon
we took turns showing each other our private
parts in the hayloft. My little sister
was there too. We didn't call it
doctor. Everyone agreed it was a fine idea.
There was no touching
until my uncle pulled back his foreskin
and edged the tiny pink head toward my little
sister. This is when the experiment came to an end.
My aunt and I were turning a corner.
My uncle and sister were hardly budding out.
Grandpa would have bellowed. My mother
would have turned red faced
then explosive. No one saw us
and later when we were grown the others
would not admit to remembering. The oldest
I have a clear sense of departing from boyhood
when I later pulled my aunt's panties
down while she slept on a feather
bed on Grandpa's living room floor. Her mound
was covered with rich dark hair and smelled
deliciously like a mix of sweet sweat and mystery.
I only wanted to know what a girl was.

Night Shift

Driving
as if my Yellow Cab
could satisfy
the ache in my headlights to see
beyond the dry mouth
of July heat lightning,
I stop and get out
squat to touch the bluegrass
that edges the curb,
and become again the boy
who climbed trees.

Four years old
I watch Dad's intent hands weave
cord around a basket
to shape a net
for the dirt court
across the street.

Twenty-one
he played guard
with the local boys.
And I sat
beneath the kitchen table
when Dad
home early from work
embraced Mom

with the news:
his promotion to
night foreman. And much
the way the tingle in reaching the top
limb of a bare sweet gum
leaves the skin in a crisp wanting
I didn't know what it meant

until years later
though since that day I
can't recall
when I last saw him
hug her
in the light.

Grandpa Rode Shotgun

on a 1924 Roadster between Georgetown, Illinois
      and Newport, Indiana. His father had taught him
how to make moonshine. In 1906 the family fled north
      after the old man shot a revenue agent in a Kentucky
tavern. A simple cobbler he had built a *still*
      to help feed his nine children.
I remember Dad hardly took a drink
      and though he had *his* temper in his blood
there was never a gun in his hand. Sundays
      we shot hay bales with a bow and arrow,
and made fun of Jesus, half-witted politicians,
      cops. Grandpa liked to box, with care he taught
his sons how to hold their fists high,
      and to strike if there was an opening
you could put a hand into. They'd start
      in the kitchen, no idea where to dance
while Grandma cleaned a squirrel
      one of the boys had just shot, or maybe
a rabbit. They'd hit, the blows hard, no reason
      to pull punches here, practice and the real thing
as close to a joke as a preacher.

Indian Summer

Everyone adores Van Gogh,
even you couched in front
of the television set
but Van Gogh
is not the subject here.

There were wild onions
in the bunch grass
across the road from
my father's country house.
And mules heehawed
on a nearby hillside.

Often I followed my shadow's
light along the trails,
and using a stick
to turn the leaves,
the neighbor kids
trudging ahead of me,
I gathered snails
in a tarnished tin cup.

He Never Smoked

In the haymow grandpa
hands his head
in his shirt pocket,
yet he never smoked
or wore loud clothing.
Even in humid weather
he refrained from
the usual sweating.
Wheels within wheels
the farmer contends
with the heat and
the fickle land's
domed silence. And still
the light begins
its falling away
from grandpa's fingers.

Our House Was Square

Our house was square and looked for all the world like the top of a grain elevator. The rent was good. My father said the house was a good house. Money was money and we had to make the best of what we had. The backyard was big. I camped there in the summer, throwing an old blanket over the clothesline, then hammering broken clothespins into each of the four corners. There were cookouts as long as warm weather lasted. And an apple tree. Red Delicious. A garden. A barrel in a far corner of the yard for trash. I still have a scar where a tin can popped its white hot lid onto my bare foot. In the fall I hung my head, no kid wanted to live in a house that looked like a box that belonged a hundred feet off the ground.

Erratum

On p. 28, l. 2, "hands" should be "hangs."

Weekends

When I was a boy I watched parents
and grandparents tear live chickens apart.
My aunt and uncle were younger than me,
so weekend visits to the farm
were full. Once on the ride back home Dad
asked Mom if she thought Grandma
and Grandpa still *danced.*
                         I winked at my sister
as a grimace flashed across her face.
I had slow danced with a girl
in Aunt Darlene's dimly lit bedroom,
danced for hours, Leslie Gore
on the phonograph
whining about the ocean
meeting the shore—I couldn't kiss the girl
though I carried her class photo
in my wallet for years.

Curfew

We had been camping out in a friend's backyard. Just an excuse, really, to run all over town after curfew. We were hungry and bored with the cold streets and unlit alleys. Our neighbor drank and drove his tired pickup around town. He owned a monkey but only because it was mean. His wife worked hard for almost no money, then there was her daughter from another marriage. She couldn't speak. She didn't attend school. It was 1963 and *special ed* hadn't come to our township. I can't remember the girl's name. She was tall. Big boned. A little heavy. When we walked up the hill to where my parents lived Larry could see the girl's bedroom light. He smirked as he crept toward her window. The girl was naked when he looked through her barely open curtains. Naked, and standing near the door to her small room. Larry began to hoot. I yelled shut-up. I was expecting Dad to return any minute from the bowling alley. It was said around old town the drunken stepfather had compromised the girl over and over. When she began to pleasure herself against the rough metal door knob, gripping the door's edge in her hand, pulling it back and forth against her dim surface, Larry pressed his lips tight to suppress a squeal, half youthful delight, half unimaginable surprise.

The Wish

We had been in the woods
for hours gathering walnuts
where we could find them. Father, Mother,

son, daughter, trampling through uncut
grasses and briars, yelling. I felt it.
Then, a field, rolling and bare,

an old apple tree near the middle,
the limbs weighted down by overripe
Jonathans, snapping with a slight touch,

into my hand. I filled my shirt,
and Mother her skirt. The day
was like a dream. I stood amazed,

I had never been
so close to fortune.
Surprise me, please,

God, somebody, I wish I could find
that person now. That other woods.
That other field. That apple tree.

Part II

Warren County Indiana

The courthouse was built from sandstone
quarried behind the old school.

A staircase of rock and a pool of slime.

Valleys, hills, roads
all of these have a blue birth.

Fall Creek Gorge carries summer to the lonely
Wabash River.

Farmers walk the early morning streets.
The town's baseball diamond stands in water.

Blue is my color: blue.

Sleepy boys slip in the river of their beds.
The firehouse alarm blares louder each night.

Welding School

The steel mill
was dark, once a man
tripped into the blast
furnace, a vat of white hot
foundry cast iron,
and was gone
in a flash of light.
One afternoon
a heavy casting fell
from a ceiling crane
used to move cast iron gear
housings through the big
building
nearly tearing off
a poor man's leg
above the knee. Dad
liked to tell how he held the
dangling limb
for the doctor
when no one else could.

The Outer Boundaries

Camel Rock and the Wilson farm
border a stone fence linked
by sultry June days and long nights,
unexpected as a teen-
age girl or the bare faces of American boys
trudging through wet farmland
in Southeast Asia. I want to know
who built the fence by the dirt road
I walked to Sulfur Springs.

There I saw Ira dive from the bank
then lift out his arm, a catfish whisker
stuck through his hand.
I sat puzzled.
What should I do with my life?
If I could see the face
stars turn to the outer boundaries
I'd put the flashlight back in my knapsack,
I'd half step the last darkening mile,

I'd hold my hands out for the light on Wilson's barn.
When I remember the Wabash River
I regret the slow way it winds down
to the lower corner of the state and
the sinewy Ohio; a plan to float
a barrel raft to New Orleans gave way

to humid August days
and cool shade,
a father's calm backyard.

Sleeping with Fire

Johnston Island, 1970

There were reconnaissance rockets
on the island, their nose cones loaded
with cameras, pointed west toward Russia,
millions apiece for ninety seconds
of photos. I slept with a pulse building
behind my eyes.

          At one launch
a man closer to the blast than me
stood frozen while the rocket
hovered just above the ground,
and as it lifted off
its long body tilting,
he turned then ran, hard,
his bones aching
for distance.

          Another thing,
one morning as I walked to the pier,
when the world struck me all at once,
I lost my bowels in a flash
of light, which explained everything,
and nothing, nothing has added up since.

Isolation

The island is want,
its streets to nowhere
shine like the ocean.

There memory showed itself
for the first time: first toy,
first shirt, first kiss—

the shadow behind chance.
Words turned into colors
mixed with ocean winds,

and slipped into themselves
when the lights dimmed out.
I felt my body turn green

free itself from the island's
half-light, then surrender
to its own dark waters.

The Rockets

There aren't enough chairs
on the island, the people, all men,
have to stand with their hands
in their pockets as the rockets
drift off the earth into the dark
sky, one man waves as if an old
friend had left him for good.

Feigning Insanity

Bremerton Naval Hospital, 1971

I can still see Ward W,
corpsmen peering

around every corner,
the Red Cross passing out apples,

teenage girls from town
singing folk songs.

Still, I dreamed of home,
and a silence pouring out

of the ground, the way
wind rips through corn rows

or winter wheat, Dad
out in his easy chair.

At last I understood how
sailing into dark harbors

had to be my dream too.
I guess 1942 was rough

for twelve year old boys
who couldn't tell a city

bus from a cow
pissing in a clover field.

The Last Summer

Light was what I wanted. Sleep was darkness.
I slept the death of a child whose body
was growing against his will. When I reached
a height of obligation I leaned into the wind,
howling one last dream said among friends.
The scare was I'd mature the way a road falls apart,
only to be repaved by workers whose names I can't say
because I never see them. In the first place I was new
but slowly my body drifted toward the trees,
and I was what everyone had said I'd become. Somewhere
on a cold road that only I can own sits
the overcoat of a soul, lost, or waiting. Awake
to nothing that isn't its own. The wish that held me
there in the place where only I can go drinks light
through a sheet of skin, a blind and innocent child.

A Dream of Water

I walk over a bridge of boards held
together by a rope on the surface
of choppy water but the bridge gives
with each step that I take. A blond woman stands
beside me. I think we made it . No
shoreline is visible. The water
is dark green. Bottomless. The notes I leave
around my apartment follow me through blank
moonless streets. They sing, "You know
what you have to do, now do it." Back on
the island I stand on the roof of the dormitory
turning in circles, a full moon shows the rim
of the Pacific to be fire. The docks
rise up and become my grandparents, they walk
into a classroom full of grade schoolers. An alarm
goes off and they all slide down a spiral
fire escape. I consider suicide, lean
over to see if I spelled it right.

Unbending Intent

It's 1987. I'm married now.
I have two boys. My hair
is shorter. I drive a Subaru.
Old friends hardly know me.
The mustache that once curled
over my delicate upper lip
is gone. Don't get me wrong, I wasn't
decadent, I was just looking
for myself in the long dark
of my early years when Dad
prodded me into his own lost dream.
He thought the way to hold
your head above the water
was to see the world in a sailor suit,
one made to order for any boy
who wanted to press his rubbery frame
into its blue lie, blue the color
of warmth, a warmth that would never
penetrate the smooth skin of desire.
No matter how gentle the wind
appeared in 1969, there was a big
lie in the air around everyone's body
in that year of riots and napalm.
Now my own boys fight;
I ask myself what can it mean?
But there's love in how they look out

for each other; then the older one
will turn on his smaller brother
like a stray animal too long on its own.
But for what I still ask myself?
A parent's attention shifts
between births almost like fashion
among those monied enough to care.
I can't follow it all, and wonder
will my boys ever see
their real father, how he told
the ship's chaplain that he wouldn't
sail when the ship left port
for the Gulf of Tonkin. Would
they understand his three months
on the psych ward feigning insanity
to avoid the craziness of a country
gone totally mad? *Unbending intent*
was my phrase, the saving grace
that steeled my blood against those
who wouldn't listen, that carried
me through to those who would.

Birds, Small Children

Provincetown, Massachusetts, 1987

I want to walk the harbor at dusk
to follow the curve of land with my eye
and remember the long drive from Oregon

how the days fall away
the way light spills out of a dream, or a boy
tags along behind a Veterans Day Parade, guns

and flags held high, violating
the blue sky of birds, small children.
I long for the Atlantic. It reminds me

of how big the world is
of how I struggle to fit into it. Death
and water are related, bonded by the invisible

dimension of time, water seeking out its
own level, with boundless ease. Water, death;
me, you; all of us, bonded and circling down,

the future told in a dust cloud long ago, a wisp of con-
densation hovering over the primordial ground,
setting the tenor for your final moment: water, destiny;

a last glimpse of the circle of fire. Minutes
tick off, water through a sieve
rushing against the infinite, the threat

of unrecorded time, the inconsolable passage, growth
and decay, now the past unravels
beside the invention of daily quotas

and the forty hour work week; madness
as dangerous as snipping the baby's umbilical cord
too soon. Bradford and Commercial Street run north

to the Atlantic, asphalt drawn to whitecaps
and blue sky, the story of a boy and the smell
of saltwater, land's end.

Distance

for Dashiell

My boy sleeps snoring on his side,
it is midday, and I'm ready for relief,
six months old he can yell Dad, or moan
Nin, Nin repeatedly, his syllable for Mom.
My upper arms are sore from lugging
him, sleeping, across town,
but I can't blame him for shrugging
off the cold with beautiful sleep.
Now his mother walks out of the shower,
she wriggles, pulling the raspberry towel
across her backside. He cries,
and the lover's bed slips farther away,
at night it floats above my head, shaking
its feathers onto my upturned face.

Simple Love

for Julian

Memories circle my body,
a lost blackbird—
I see my father

when I yell at my son. He's
sluggish in the morning,
not slow-witted,

just a little
too willing to let the events
of the day unfold

without him. I'm
for his struggle,
I see him attentive

in my daydreams.
I want to be as cunning
as the rudder

of a sailboat. I'll
tack the corners
of his angry heart. I'll

walk ahead of him
with a bag of tricks. I'll
turn his eyes inward

where he'll find
strength. I'll yell
from the crow's nest

of his soul for him
to open his arms
to the double world

of mirrors.

I Want, I Want

for Julian and Dashiell

It is late July, 1986
and I can't keep my son
out of the trees, I want,

I want, his favorite
saying. Pop, he started
calling me Pop shortly

before he turned three,
no warning, just his face
turned up toward mine.

He sleeps now, as does
his younger brother,
the one with my face, everything

goes into his mouth,
grass, rocks, toy trucks,
the garden pea unfolding into

a loon while I walk
behind him, picking up
the mysterious, the chewed

pieces left for spring
dark to reclaim, winter
rests at the end

of his sure hands, hands that
touch slowly like morning's
first crack of light. These

are the years I have
lived my life for, giving
each breath back in exchange

for another step, and this
silence turning in my mind
as they turn in their sleep.

I Could Be Wrong

Someone has to do the dirty dishes.
It's not like I was asked to do something
useless. Every time a used cup appears

on the counter
or a knife with a pad of peanut butter
is left in the sink

I know someone is thinking of me.
What could be better than this?
It's not as if I were being drafted.

I could be a prisoner
falsely accused of an unimaginable crime.
Life is almost too easy here.

I could be wrong. It hasn't rained in weeks.
Things at a distance
seem to be shifting. If you look

you can see the waves of heat lifting
off the fields.

Bloom and Bloom and Bloom

I picked wild flowers at a rest park
in Wyoming, tied them to the rear view mirror
to remind myself where I'd been,

Truckers roared past me in the dead of night,
I practiced courtesy, dimming my lights,
slowing so they'd know I wanted them to pass.

The radio wouldn't play in the Rockies,
so I drove with the vents open
and the windows down, into Nebraska.

I drove for hours without saying a word,
slept without dreaming. In the morning farms
in Iowa and Illinois were a blur. But that night

I saw him, Dad, shirtless, in dim porch light,
holding the screen door open, welcoming me
after ten long years, with a look.

He's thin now, thinner than I'd imagined,
two lines sweep across his barrel chest,
there's a third along the base of his neck,

where a doctor, a stranger to me, has done his work.
But there, in the doorway, Dad's eyes glowed,
they glowed wild and calm at once,

their light dissolving the years and the distances
I'd put between us, dissolving the war and miles
of interstate and mountains and prairie. The

flowers from along the interstate bloom and bloom and bloom
as if out of their own ashes,
or their own forgotten past that will not die.

With My Sons

Provincetown, Massachusetts, 1988

I watch waves curl
onto the sandy beach
at Race Point. Sometimes

I have to hold the older one,
he's pulled closer, he says,
excited and fearless,

as each wave crashes
before him. I'd say he's
drawn to the enormity

of the mysterious by the way he tugs
against my steady grip,
saying let me go, Papa,

let me go, I'm wearing
my rubber boots, but I
pull him back from each wave,

and he laughs,
dragging his boot heels
in the sand.

Thoughts on the Seven Year Itch

In the beginning I loved my wife,
and she loved me, opening the gates
to her passion, giving of herself
and taking, in turn, from me, that which
I had to give. But the years wear us down,
and the children, and the responsibilities
curb the fire, set the mind to thinking.
There's danger in freedom, desire the last
thing you want to leave behind when you leave
the house. The day comes as the front porch
fades from sight, and the days tumble over one
another like the pile of dirty clothes
by the bidet. The street outside is gravel,
a cul-de-sac where the neighbors build their fences
flush against the street, guarding every inch
of their bought and paid for freedom. I dream
about the beach on the Atlantic side of the Cape,
debris and waves crashing together onto the shore,
a legacy of sadness like the millstone marriage brings
to those with weak hearts; saltwater and sea air,
tightly rolled joints, autoeroticism, all of these help,
if only a little, in the half-light of dreamy
daytime thoughts of romance and meeting someone new.
In the end it doesn't add up, or even need to.

History

I walk into the warehouse,
the ceiling heater rages,

the early morning chill
still holds the big room. Overhead

the pipe for the walk-in freezer drips,
the warehouse cat meows at my heels.

I should know what to do?
I turn on the radio as the newscaster

tells everyone the war in Iraq,
though over weeks ago, has pockets

of resistance. I remember each word
my Chaucer professor spoke

when he asked class what war is.
No one raised their hand. *War*

is men killing men, he said, *war*
is men killing men. Real work

begins in the long dark, lonely
against the backdrop of ordinary days.

When I Walk the Path I've Worn

between the warehouse and the store
my past and future collide
like a bad carnival ride. My hand truck
is heavy with regret, lost hours,
days sprinkled with the dark foot
of micromanagement. I watch the cashiers
who are talking again, talking and asking cus-
tomers if they're enjoying their day. One
of the younger cashiers wears
an *illegal* shirt; her beautiful arm-
pits are revealed in all their tender
glory. I can hear a delivery truck
rumbling down the scarred
gravel alleyway. I try to think of labor
as a kind of workout. Meanwhile the
truck driver is grousing about routing
again. The general manager com-
plains about payroll. New workers
are sluggish, awash in the hurry of barely enough.

Things Left Unsaid

for Edward Moody, 1930-1988

Soft cries from a nearby nursery
fill my father's hospital room.
For a moment he has a new life.

I rub his back
whenever the morphine
drifts off. He complains

because he is tired of seeing things
he doesn't want to see. He tells me
he already knows everything

he needs to know. When the drug
splashes into his bloodstream
he goes back to the steel mill,

sits up in his bed to twist imaginary gauges,
then asking for chalk shouts orders
to his men. When the doctors

said nothing could be done
he settled into a good humor.
Near the end

home was all he wanted. Home.
A grinding Midwestern winter,
a stiff wind, and a snowstorm.

The Tender Mounds

The long drive home was like a paper cut.

The interstate had been swallowed by fog
and the big trucks.

I could almost see the dark outline
of cows in the clover fields.

On nights such as this there's something to be said
for strong fences; but there's no way to get even in this life.

The darkness builds and builds

until one day you're swimming along
and a log bumps the tender mounds

under your scalp. Things could be better.
I still want to reach into the city of my body

and find a star. Last night
I could hear the 3:30 a.m. freight train

rumbling through town,
its lonely whistle as clear as death.

Simple Language

Clouds hide the deep blue
the little-known river

that trails us all.
I try to connect the stars

to the gestures.
We are trapped, but this we know

or should. When it rains
it is the ghosts

of our parents crying,
crying because

their loving tongues
can no longer warn us

that the days
dim or bright

are the days.

Acknowledgments

Some of the poems in this manuscript have appeared in the following publications:

Café Solo: "Simple Language." *Caliban*: "Memory is the Rig" under the title "Untitled." *Clackamas Literary Review*: "With My Sons." *Dislocate Literary Journal*: "Welding School." *Eclipse*: "The Experiment." Fireweed: "Birds, Small Children," "I Could Be Wrong" and "Sleeping with Fire." *Hubbub*: "The Rockets." *Indiana Review*: "The Last Summer." the *Kerf*: "Grandma." *Mississippi Mud*: "Isolation" and "The Wish." *Mudfish*: "Bloom and Bloom and Bloom, " "Weekends" and "Thoughts on the Seven Year Itch." *Paragraph*: "Our House Was Square." *Permafrost*: "Night Shift." *Pleiades*: "Warren County Indiana." *Raven Chronicles*: "The Novice." *Riverwind*: "Grandpa Rode Shotgun." *Shankpainter*: "Distance" and "Feigning Insanity." *Snapdragon*: "I Want, I Want" and "He Never Smoked." *Skidrow Penthouse*: "The Tender Mounds." *South Dakota Review*: "Indian Summer" and "Summer Winds." *The Southern Poetry Review*: "Unbending Intent." *Stringtown*: "The Woods." *Talus & Scree*: "Things Left Unsaid." *upstreet*: "History" and "When I Walk the Path I've Worn." *Willow Springs*: "Your Eyes Your Tongue Your Baptist Church." *Wind*: "The Outer Boundaries" under the title "Searching Out the Past." *ZYZZYVA*: "Simple Love."

"Distance" and "The Rockets" were reprinted in *The Oregonian*, Portland, Oregon.

Some of the poems in this book appeared in the chapbooks *Unbending Intent* (26 Books, 1996) and *Bloom and Bloom and Bloom* (sight | for | sight books, 2013).

"Distance" was reprinted in *Cape Discovery, The Provincetown Fine Arts Work Center Anthology*, Sheep Meadow Press, 1994.

"Night Shift" was reprinted in *From Here We Speak: An Anthology of Oregon Poetry*, Oregon State University Press, 1993.

"He Never Smoked" was reprinted in *The Anthology of Eugene Writers #1*, Northwest Review Books, 1982.

In 2013 "Simple Language" was reprinted as a letterpress broadside by Wood Works.

The author wishes to thank the Fine Arts Work Center in Provincetown, Massachusetts for Fellowships in 1983-1984 and 1987-1988 during which time many of these poems were written.

About the Author

Rodger Moody is the founding editor of Silverfish Review Press. Poems have appeared in many magazines, including *Caliban, Cloudbank, upstreet, Indiana Review, Paragraph, Mudfish*, and *ZYZZYVA*. He has been a writing fellow at the Fine Arts Work Center in Provincetown, Massachusetts. In 2012 he received a writing fellowship from Literary Arts in Portland, Oregon. *Self-Portrait / Sixteen Sevenlings* received the 2012 At Hand Chapbook Award from Bright Hill Press of Treadwell, NY. A second chapbook, *Bloom and Bloom and Bloom*, was released in 2013 by sight | for | sight books. For the past twenty-nine years he has made his living as a warehouse worker.

This book was set in Adobe Jenson, a faithful electronic version of the 1470 roman face of Nicolas Jenson. Jenson was a Frenchman employed as the mintmaster at Tours. Legend has it that he was sent to Mainz in 1458 by Charles VII to learn the new art of printing in the shop of Gutenberg, and import it to France. But he never returned, appearing in Venice in 1468; there his first roman types appeared, in his edition of Eusebius. He moved to Rome at the invitation of Pope Sixtus IV, where he died in 1480.

Type historian Daniel Berkeley Updike praises the Jenson Roman for "its readability, its mellowness of form, and the evenness of color in mass." Updike concludes, "Jenson's roman types have been the accepted models for roman letters ever since he made them, and, repeatedly copied in our own day, have never been equalled."

sight | for | sight books is committed to preserving ancient forests and natural resources. We elected to print *History* on 30% post consumer recycled paper, processed chlorine free. As a result, for this printing, we have saved: 1 tree (40' tall and 6-8" diameter), 499 gallons of water, 293 kilowatt hours of electricity, 64 pounds of solid waste, and 120 pounds of greenhouse gases. Thomson-Shore, Inc. is a member of Green Press Initiative, a nonprofit program dedicated to supporting authors, publishers, and suppliers in their efforts to reduce their use of fiber obtained from endangered forests. For more information, visit www.greenpressinitiative.org.

Cover design by Valerie Brewster, Scribe Typography
Text design by Rodger Moody and Connie Kudura, ProtoType
Printed on acid-free papers and bound by Thomson-Shore, Inc.